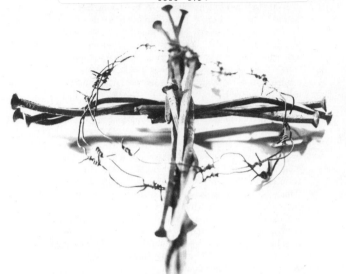

He Did This Just for You

MAX LUCADO

W PUBLISHING GROUP™
www.wpublishinggroup.com

A Division of Thomas Nelson, Inc.
www.ThomasNelson.com

HE DID THIS JUST FOR YOU

Unless otherwise indicated, Scripture quotations are from the Holy Bible, *New Century Version*, copyright © 1987, 1988, 1991 by W Publishing Group, Nashville, TN. Used by permission. Those marked NLT are taken from the Holy Bible, *New Living Translation*, copyright © 1996. Used by permission of Tyndale House Publishers, Inc., Wheaton, Illinois 60187. All rights reserved. Other Scripture references are from the following sources:
The Holy Bible, *New International Version* (NIV). Copyright © 1973, 1978, 1984, International Bible Society. Used by permission of Zondervan Bible Publishers. *The Living Bible* (TLB), copyright © 1971 by Tyndale House Publishers, Wheaton, Ill. Used by permission. *The Message* (MSG), copyright © 1993. Used by permission of NavPress Publishing Group. The *New King James Version* (NKJV), copyright © 1979, 1980, 1982, Thomas Nelson, Inc., Publisher. The *New Revised Standard Version* Bible (NRSV), © 1989 by the Division of Christian Education of the National Council of the Churches of Christ in the USA. The *Contemporary English Version* (CEV) © 1991 by the American Bible Society. Used by permission. The *New American Standard Bible* (NASB), © The Lockman Foundation 1960, 1962, 1963, 1968, 1971, 1972, 1973, 1975, 1977. Used by permission.
Much of the content of this book is taken from previously published works. Consult the permissions page in the back of the book for a complete list.
Produced with the assistance of The Livingstone Corporation. Project staff includes Paige Drygas, Dave Veerman, Christopher D. Hudson, Ashley Taylor.
ISBN 0-8499-1683-6
Printed in the United States of America.
03 04 05 PHX 15

CONTENTS

Dear Friend,

When you think of the cross, what thoughts come to mind? Steeples? Gold necklaces? Churches?

Or do your thoughts go deeper? Do words like these come to mind? Jesus. Nails. Blood. Pain. Death. Tomb. *Tomb?* Empty. Joy. Promise. Life. Savior!

Oh, the words of the cross, so full of *pain*. So full of *passion*. So full of *promise*. God's promise. His promise to you. His promise to do whatever it takes to save your soul.

By the way, that's where his thoughts are. He is thinking about you. And as you ponder the cross, he wants you to know— he did it for you. He did it just for you.

Blessings,
Max Lucado

The Parable

*"God loved the world so much that he gave his one and only
Son so that whoever believes in him may not be lost, but
have eternal life. God did not send his Son into the world to
judge the world guilty, but to save the world through him."*
John 3:16, 17 (NCV)

The Parable

Five-year-old Madeline climbed into her father's lap.

"Did you have enough to eat?" he asked her.

She smiled and patted her tummy. "I can't eat any more."

"Did you have some of your grandma's pie?"

"A whole piece!"

Joe looked across the table at his mom. "Looks like you filled us up. Don't think we'll be able to do anything tonight but go to bed."

Madeline put her little hands on either side of his big face. "Oh, but, Poppa, this is

9

Christmas Eve. You said we could dance."

Joe feigned a poor memory. "Did I now? Why, I don't remember saying anything about dancing."

Grandma smiled and shook her head as she began clearing the table.

"But, Poppa," Madeline pleaded, "we always dance on Christmas Eve. Just you and me, remember?"

A smile burst from beneath his thick mustache. "Of course I remember, darling. How could I forget?"

And with that he stood and took her hand in his, and for a moment, just a moment, his wife was alive again, and the two were walking into the den to spend another night before Christmas as they had spent so many, dancing away the evening.

They would have danced the rest of their lives, but then came the surprise pregnancy and the complications. Madeline survived. But her mother did not. And Joe, the thick-handed butcher from Minnesota, was left to raise his Madeline alone.

"Come on, Poppa." She tugged on his

hand. *"Let's dance before everyone arrives."*
She was right. Soon the doorbell would ring
and the relatives would fill the floor and the
night would be past.

But, for now, it was just Poppa and
Madeline.

GOD'S AMAZING LOVE

The love of a parent for a child is a mighty
force. Consider the couple with their new-
born child. The infant offers his parents
absolutely nothing. No money. No skill.
No words of wisdom. If he had pockets,
they would be empty. To see an infant lying
in a bassinet is to see utter helplessness.
What is there to love?

Whatever it is, Mom and Dad find it.
Just look at Mom's face as she nurses her
baby. Just watch Dad's eyes as he cradles
the child. And just try to harm or speak
evil of the infant. If you do, you'll
encounter a mighty strength, for the love

of a parent is a mighty force.

Jesus once asked, if we humans who are sinful have such a love, how much more does God, the sinless and selfless Father, love us?[1] But what happens when the love isn't returned? What happens to the heart of the father when his child turns away?

※ ※ ※

Rebellion flew into Joe's world like a Minnesota blizzard. About the time she was old enough to drive, Madeline decided she was old enough to lead her life. And that life did not include her father.

"I should have seen it coming," Joe would later say, "but for the life of me I didn't." He didn't know what to do. He didn't know how to handle the pierced nose and the tight shirts. He didn't understand the late nights and the poor grades. And, most of all, he didn't know when to speak and when to be quiet.

She, on the other hand, had it all figured out. She knew when to speak to her father— never. She knew when to be quiet—always.

The pattern was reversed, however, with the lanky, tattooed kid from down the street. He was no good, and Joe knew it.

And there was no way he was going to allow his daughter to spend Christmas Eve with that kid.

"You'll be with us tonight, young lady. You'll be at your grandma's house eating your grandma's pie. You'll be with us on Christmas Eve."

Though they were at the same table, they might as well have been on different sides of town. Madeline played with her food and said nothing. Grandma tried to talk to Joe, but he was in no mood to chat. Part of him was angry; part of him was heartbroken. And the rest of him would have given anything to know how to talk to this girl who once sat on his lap.

Soon the relatives arrived, bringing with them a welcome end to the awkward silence. As the room filled with noise and people, Joe stayed on one side, Madeline sat sullenly on the other.

"Put on the music, Joe," reminded one of

*his brothers. And so he did. Thinking she
would be honored, he turned and walked
toward his daughter. "Will you dance with
your Poppa tonight?"*

*The way she huffed and turned, you'd
have thought he'd insulted her. In full view of
the family, she walked out the front door and
marched down the sidewalk. Leaving her
father alone.*

Very much alone.

GOD'S ENEMIES

According to the Bible, we have done the
same. We have spurned the love of our
Father. "Each of us has gone his own way"
(Isaiah 53:6, NCV).

The apostle Paul takes our rebellion a
step further. We have done more than turn
away, he says; we have turned *against* our
Father. "We were living against God"
(Romans 5:6, NCV).

He speaks even more bluntly later,

when he says, "We were God's enemies" (Romans 5:10). Harsh words, don't you think? An enemy is a hostile adversary. One who offends, not out of ignorance, but by intent. Does this describe us? Have we ever been enemies of God? Have we ever turned against our Father?

Have you . . .

ever done something, knowing God wouldn't want you to do it?

ever hurt one of his children or part of creation?

ever supported or applauded the work of his adversary, the devil?

ever turned against your heavenly Father in public?

If so, have you not taken the role of an enemy?

According to the Bible, we are "by nature children of wrath" (Ephesians 2:3, NASB). It is not that we *can't* do good. We do. It's just that we can't keep from doing bad.

"There is none righteous, not even one . . . All have sinned and fall short of the glory of God" (Romans 3:10, 23, NASB).

Some would disagree with such strong words. They look around and say, "Compared to everyone else, I'm a decent person." You know, a pig might say something similar. He might look at his trough-partners and announce, "I'm just as clean as everyone else." Compared to humans, however, that pig needs help. Compared to God, we humans need the same. The standard for sinlessness isn't found at the pig troughs of the earth but at the throne of heaven. God himself is the standard.

Our God is a perfect God, untainted by sin, untethered by mistakes. Where we see nothing but murky waters, he sees nothing but purity. Where we dwell in darkness, he dwells in light. God has never sinned.

And we have never *not* sinned. God has lived a sinless eternity; I'd be thrilled with a sinless hour! But I've never had one. Have you? Have you ever gone sixty minutes with only one sin? Me neither. But for the sake of contrast, let's say you did. Let's say you lived a life in which you averaged only one sin an hour. Shall we do the math? An average life span of 72 years would mean 630,720 sins. Since you're reading this book, let's round it down to 600,000.

Now envision the moment you stand before God. He is a perfect God, remember, and heaven is a perfect place. And you? You would be perfect, too, except for the 600,000 failures on your record. Separating you and God is an insurmountable flood of imperfection and sin.

We have a problem: We are sinners, and God says "the wages of sin is death" (Romans 6:23, NASB).

What can we do? How does God react when we become his enemies?

   ⸺   ⸺   ⸺

Madeline came back that night but not for long. Joe never faulted her for leaving. After all, what's it like being the daughter of a butcher? In their last days together he tried so hard. He made her favorite dinner—she didn't want to eat. He invited her to a movie—she just stayed in her room. He bought her a new dress—she didn't even say thank you. And then there was that spring day he left work early to be at the house when she arrived home from school.

Wouldn't you know that was the day she never came home.

A friend saw her and her boyfriend in the vicinity of the bus station. The authorities confirmed the purchase of a ticket to Chicago; where she went from there was any-body's guess.

THE WAY HOME

The most notorious road in the world is the Via Dolorosa, "the Way of Sorrows." According to tradition, it is the route Jesus took from Pilate's hall to Calvary. The path is marked by stations frequently used by Christians for their devotions. One station marks the passing of Pilate's verdict. Another, the appearance of Simon to carry the cross. Two stations commemorate the stumble of Christ, another the words of

Christ. There are fourteen stations in all,
each one a reminder of the events of
Christ's final journey.

Is the route accurate? Probably not.
When Jerusalem was destroyed in A.D. 70
and again in A.D. 135, the streets of the city
were destroyed. As a result, no one knows
the exact route Christ followed that Friday.

But we do know where the path actually
began.

The path began, not in the court of
Pilate, but in the halls of heaven. The
Father began his journey when he left his
home in search of us. Armed with nothing
more than a passion to win your heart, he
came looking.

This is the heart of the Christian message. God became a human. He was born
in an ordinary stable to ordinary parents.
But his was an extraordinary purpose. He
came to take us to heaven. His death was a
sacrifice for our sins. Jesus was our substi-
tute. He paid for our mistakes so we
wouldn't have to. Jesus' desire was singu-
lar—to bring his children home. The Bible

has a word for this quest: *reconciliation*.

"God was in Christ reconciling the world to Himself" (2 Corinthians 5:19, NKJV). The Greek word for *reconcile* means "to render something otherwise."[2] The path to the cross tells us exactly how far God will go to put it back together. Reconciliation restitches the unraveled, reverses the rebellion, rekindles the cold passion.

Reconciliation touches the shoulder of the wayward and woos him homeward.

The scrawny boy with the tattoos had a cousin. The cousin worked the night shift at a convenience store south of Houston. For a few bucks a month, he would let the runaways stay in his apartment at night, but they had to be out during the day.

Which was fine with them. They had big plans. He was going to be a mechanic, and Madeline just knew she could get a job at a department store. Of course he knew nothing

about cars, and she knew even less about getting a job—but you don't think of things like
that when you're intoxicated on freedom.

After a couple of weeks, the cousin
changed his mind. And the day he announced
his decision, the boyfriend announced his.
Madeline found herself facing the night with
no place to sleep or hand to hold.

It was just the first of many such nights.

A woman in the park told her about the
homeless shelter near the bridge. For a couple of bucks she could get a bowl of soup and
a cot. A couple of bucks was about all she
had. She used her backpack as a pillow and
jacket as a blanket. The room was so rowdy
it was hard to sleep. Madeline turned her face
to the wall and, for the first time in several
days, thought of the whiskered face of her
father kissing her goodnight. But as her eyes
began to water, she refused to cry. She pushed
the memory deep inside and determined not
to think about home.

She'd gone too far to go back.

The next morning, the girl in the cot
beside her showed her a fistful of tips she'd

made from dancing on tables. "This is the last night I'll have to stay here," she said. "Now I can pay for my own place. They told me they are looking for another girl. You should come by." She reached into her pocket and pulled out a matchbook. "Here's the address."

Madeline's stomach turned at the thought. All she could do was mumble, "I'll think about it."

She spent the rest of the week on the streets looking for work. At the end of the week when it was time to pay her bill at the shelter, she reached into her pocket and pulled out the matchbook. It was all she had left.

"I won't be staying tonight," she said and walked out the door.

Hunger has a way of softening convictions.

PRIDE AND SHAME

Pride and shame. You'd never know they are sisters. They appear so different. Pride

puffs out her chest. Shame hangs her head.
Pride boasts. Shame hides. Pride seeks to be
seen. Shame seeks to be avoided.

But don't be fooled, the emotions have
the same parentage. And the emotions have
the same impact. They keep you from your
Father.

Pride says, "You're too good for him."

Shame says, "You're too bad for him."

Pride drives you away.

Shame keeps you away.

If pride is what goes before a fall, then
shame is what keeps you from getting up
after one.

*If Madeline knew anything, she knew how
to dance. Her father had taught her. Now men
the age of her father watched her. She didn't
rationalize it—she just didn't think about it.
Madeline simply did her work and took their
dollars.*

*She might have never thought about it,
except for the letters. The cousin brought
them. Not one, or two, but a box full. All*

23

addressed to her. All from her father.

"Your old boyfriend must have squealed on you. These come two or three a week," complained the cousin. "Give him your address." Oh, but she couldn't do that. He might find her.

Nor could she bear to open the envelopes. She knew what they said; he wanted her home. But if he knew what she was doing, he would not be writing.

It seemed less painful not to read them. So she didn't. Not that week, nor the next when the cousin brought more, nor the next when he came again. She kept them in the dressing room at the club, organized according to postmark. She ran her finger over the top of each but couldn't bear to open one.

Most days Madeline was able to numb the emotions. Thoughts of home and thoughts of shame were shoved into the same part of her heart. But there were occasions when the thoughts were too strong to resist.

Like the time she saw a dress in the clothing store window. A dress the same color as the one her father had purchased for her. A

dress that had been far too plain for her. With much reluctance she had put it on and stood with him before the mirror. "My, you are as tall as I am," he had told her. She had stiffened at his touch.

Seeing her weary face reflected in the store window, Madeline realized she'd give a thousand dresses to feel his arm again. She left the store and resolved not to pass by it again.

CHOICES

We all make choices. Sometimes wisely, sometimes not. God gives eternal choices, and these choices have eternal consequences.

You've made some bad choices in life, haven't you? You've chosen the wrong friends, maybe the wrong career, even the wrong spouse. You look back over your life and say, "If only . . . if only I could make up for those bad choices." You can. One good choice for eternity offsets a thousand bad ones on earth. The choice is yours.

Since Jesus came to earth, this eternal

choice has been available to us. And yet we wonder how some can choose eternal life and some reject it. We wonder how two men can see the same Jesus, and one choose to mock him and the other choose to pray to him. I don't know how, but they did.

That's what happened at the cross. There were two other crosses on the hill that day, the day that Jesus died. Two criminals, suffering the same death. And those two crosses remind us of one of God's greatest gifts: the gift of choice. One chose Jesus; the other merely mocked him. Scripture reveals a compelling part of the story:

One of the criminals on a cross began to shout insults at Jesus: "Aren't you the king of the Jews? Then save yourself and us." But the other criminal stopped him and said, "You should fear God! You are getting the same punishment he is. We are punished justly, getting what we deserve for what we did. But this man has done nothing wrong." Then he said, "Jesus, remem-

ber me when you come into your king-
dom." Jesus said to him, "I tell you the
truth, today you will be with me in par-
adise" (Luke 23:39–43, NIV).

When one dying criminal prayed, Jesus
loved him enough to save him. And when
the other mocked, Jesus loved him
enough to let him.

He allowed him the choice.

He does the same for you.

*In time the leaves fell and the air chilled.
The mail came and the cousin complained
and the stack of letters grew. Still she refused
to send him an address. And she refused to
read a letter.*

*Then a few days before Christmas Eve
another letter arrived. Same shape. Same
color. But this one had no postmark. And it
was not delivered by the cousin. It was sit-
ting on her dressing room table.*

*"A couple of days ago a big man stopped
by and asked me to give this to you,"*

explained one of the other dancers. "Said you'd understand the message."

"He was here?" she asked anxiously.

The woman shrugged, "Suppose he had to be."

Madeline swallowed hard and looked at the envelope. She opened it and removed the card. "I know where you are," it read. "I know what you do. This doesn't change the way I feel. What I've said in each letter is still true."

"But I don't know what you've said," Madeline declared. She pulled a letter from the top of the stack and read it. Then a second and a third. Each letter had the same exact sentence. Each sentence asked the same question.

In a matter of moments the floor was littered with paper, and her face was streaked with tears.

Within an hour she was on a bus. "I just might make it in time."

She barely did.

The relatives were starting to leave. Joe was helping Grandma in the kitchen when his brother called from the suddenly quiet den. "Joe, someone is here to see you."

Joe stepped out of the kitchen and stopped. In one hand the girl held a backpack. In the other she held a card. He saw the question in her eyes.

"The answer is 'yes,'" she said to her father. "If the invitation is still good, the answer is 'yes.'"

Joe swallowed hard. "Oh my. The invitation is good."

And so the two danced again on Christmas Eve.

On the floor, near the door, rested a letter with Madeline's name and her father's request.

"Will you come home and dance with your Poppa again?"

The Promise

The Promise

*T*he cross. Can you turn any direction without seeing one? Perched atop a chapel. Carved into a graveyard headstone. Engraved into a ring or suspended on a chain. The cross is the universal symbol of Christianity. An odd choice, don't you think? Strange that a tool of torture would come to embody a movement of hope. The symbols of other faiths are more upbeat: the six-pointed star of Jerusalem, the crescent moon of Islam, a lotus blossom for Buddhism. Yet a cross for Christianity? An instrument of execution?

Would you wear a tiny electric chair around your neck? Suspend a gold-plated hangman's noose on the wall? Would you print a picture of a firing squad on a business card? Yet we do so with the cross. Many even make the sign of the cross as they pray. Would we make the sign of, say, a guillotine? Instead of the triangular touch on the forehead and shoulders, how about a karate chop on the palm? Doesn't quite have the same feel, does it?

Why is the cross the symbol of our faith? To find the answer, look no further than the cross itself. Its design couldn't be simpler. One beam horizontal, the other vertical. One reaches out like God's love. The other reaches up as does God's holiness. One represents the width of his love, the other reflects the height of his holiness. The cross is the intersection of both. The cross is where God forgave his children without lowering his standard.

How could he do this? In a sentence: God put our sin on his Son and punished it there.

"God put on him the wrong who never did anything wrong, so we could be put right with God" (2 Corinthians 5:21, MSG).

Or as another version reads, "Christ never sinned! But God treated him as a sinner, so that Christ could make us acceptable to God" (2 Corinthians 5:21, CEV).

Envision the moment. God on his throne. You on the earth. And between you and God, suspended between you and heaven, is Christ on his cross. Your sins have been placed on Jesus. God, who punishes sin, releases his rightful wrath on your mistakes. Jesus receives the blow. Since Christ is between you and God, you don't. The sin is punished, but you are safe, safe in the shadow of the cross.

This is what God did, but why, why would he do it? Moral duty? Heavenly obligation? Paternal requirement? No. God is required to do nothing.

Besides, consider what he did. He gave his Son. His only Son. Would you do that? Would you offer the life of your child for someone else? I wouldn't. There are those for whom I would give my life. But ask me to make a list of those for whom I would kill my daughter. The sheet will be blank. I don't need a pencil. The list has no names.

But God's list contains the name of every person who ever lived. For this is the scope of his love. And this is the reason for the cross. He loves the world.

"For God so loved the world that he gave his only Son . . ." (John 3:16, NLT).

As boldly as the center beam proclaims God's holiness, the crossbeam declares his love. And, oh, how wide his love reaches.

Aren't you glad the verse does not read:

"For God so loved the rich . . ."?

Or, "For God so loved the famous . . ."?

Or, "For God so loved the thin . . ."?

It doesn't. Nor does it state, "For God so loved the Europeans or Africans . . ." ". . . the sober or successful . . ." ". . . the young or the old . . ."

No, when we read John 3:16, we simply (and happily) read, "For God so loved the world . . . ."

How wide is God's love? Wide enough for the whole world. Are you included in the world? Then you are included in God's love.

It's nice to be included. You aren't always. Universities exclude you if you aren't smart enough. Businesses exclude you if you aren't qualified enough, and sadly, some churches exclude you if you aren't good enough.

But though they may exclude you, Christ includes you. When asked to describe the width of his love, he stretched one hand to the right and the other to the left and had them nailed in that position so you would know, he died loving you.

The Privilege

GOD'S INVITATION TO YOU

The Privilege

GOD'S INVITATION TO YOU

I can remember, as a seven-year-old, going to my grand-parents' house for a week. Mom and Dad bought a ticket, gave me some spending money, put me on a Greyhound bus, and told me not to talk to strangers or get off the bus until I saw my grandma out the window. They made it very clear to me that my destiny was Ralls, Texas.

God has done the same for you. He has placed you on a journey. He has a destiny for your life (and you'll be glad to know it's not Ralls, Texas).

"For God has destined us not for wrath but for obtaining salvation through our Lord Jesus Christ" (1 Thessalonians 5:9, NRSV).

According to the Bible, God's destiny for your life is salvation. Your intended destination is heaven. God has done exactly what my parents did. He has purchased your passage. He has equipped you for the journey. God loves you so much that he wants you to be with him forever.

The choice, however, is up to you. Even though he stands at the door with ticket paid and pocket money for the trip . . . many choose to go in directions other than the one God intends. That is the problem.

OUR PROBLEM: SIN
(WE'RE ON THE WRONG BUS)

When my parents gave me the ticket and told me which bus to board, I believed them and did what they said. I trusted them. I knew they loved me, and I knew they knew more than I did . . . so I got on board.

Becoming a Christian is getting on board with Christ. Jesus stands at the door of the bus and says, "I am the way, the truth, and the life. No one comes to the Father except through Me" (John 14:6, NKJV). Unfortunately, not all accept his invitation. I know I didn't the first time he invited. I spent some time on the wrong bus.

There are many buses, each of them promising to take you to happiness. There is the bus of pleasure, possessions, power, passion. I saw a bus called *party* and got on board. It was full of people laughing and carousing; they seemed to be enjoying a nonstop party. It was quite some time before I learned they had to be loud to cover up all the pain inside.

The word for getting on the wrong bus is *sin*. Sin is when we say, *I'll go my way instead of God's way.* Right in the middle of the word *sin* is the word *I*. Sin is when we say, *I'll do what I want, no matter what God says.* Only God can fulfill our needs. Sin is the act of going to everyone but God for what only God can give. Am I the only one who has spent time on the wrong bus? No. Some buses are more violent than others. Some rides are more lengthy than others but:

"All of us like sheep have gone astray, each of us has turned to his own way" (Isaiah 53:6, NASB).

"If we say that we have no sin, we are only fooling ourselves, and refusing to accept the truth" (1 John 1:8, TLB).

"We're sinners, every one of us, in the same sinking boat with everybody else" (Romans 3:20, MSG).

To board the wrong bus is a serious mistake. Sin breaks our relationship with God. We were intended to journey with him. But when we are on a different bus headed the wrong direction, we feel far from God. This is why life can seem so cruddy. We aren't fulfilling our destiny.

Sin not only breaks our relationship with God, it also hampers our relationships with others. Can you imagine taking a long trip to the wrong place with a busload of people? With time, everyone gets cranky. Nobody likes the trip. The journey is miserable.

We try to cope with the problems by therapy or recreation or prescriptions. But nothing helps. The Bible says:

"There is a path before each person that seems right, but it ends in death" (Proverbs 16:25, NLT).

You see, the end result of sin is death . . . spiritual death. "The wages of sin," Paul writes, "is death . . ." (Romans 6:23, NIV). Spend a life on the wrong bus headed in the wrong direction, and you'll end up in the wrong place. You'll end up in hell. Not because God wants you in hell. His plan for you is heaven. Your destiny is heaven. He'll do anything to get you to heaven, with one exception. There is one thing he won't do. He won't force you. The decision is yours. But he has done everything else. Let me show you what I mean.

THE SOLUTION: GRACE
(GO TO THE RIGHT BUS)

If the problem is sin and all have sinned, what can you do? Well, you can go to church, but that won't make you a Christian. Just like going to a rodeo doesn't make you a cowboy, going to church doesn't make you a Christian. You could work really hard to please God. You could do a lot of good stuff, give away a lot of things . . . the only problem with that is that you don't know how many good things you have to do. Or you could compare yourself with others: "I may be bad, but at least I'm better than Hitler." The problem with comparisons is that other people aren't the standard; God is!

So what are you going to do? If you aren't saved by going to church or doing good works or by comparing yourself to others, how are you saved? The answer is simple: Go to the right bus.

"For God so loved the world that he

gave his one and only Son, that whoever believes in him shall not perish but have eternal life" (John 3:16, NIV).

Note what God did: " . . . He gave his only Son." This is how he dealt with your sin. Imagine it this way. Suppose you are found guilty of a crime. You are in a courtroom in front of the judge, and he sentences you to death for your crime. His sentence is just. You are guilty, and the punishment for your crime is death. But suppose that the judge is your father. He knows the law; he knows that your crime demands a death. But he knows love; he knows that he loves you too much to let you die. So in a wonderful act of love, he stands and removes his robe and stands by your side and says, "I'm going to die in your place."

That is what God did for you. The wages of sin is death. Heaven's justice demands a death for your sin. Heaven's love, however, can't bear to see you die. So here is what God did. He stood and removed his heavenly robes. He came to earth to tell us that he would die for us. He would be our Savior. And that is what he did.

"God put the world square with himself through the Messiah, giving the world a fresh start by offering forgiveness of sins . . . God put on him the wrong who never did anything wrong, so we could be put right with God" (2 Corinthians 5:19,21, MSG).

THE RESPONSE: TRUST
(GETTING ON THE RIGHT BUS)

What does God want you to do? He wants you to get on his bus. How is this done? Three simple steps: admit, agree, accept.

1. *Admit* that God has not been first place in your life, and ask him to forgive your sins.

"If we confess our sins to him, he is faithful and just to forgive us and to cleanse us from every wrong" (1 John 1:9, NLT).

2. *Agree* that Jesus died to pay for your sins and that he rose from the dead and is alive today.

"If you confess with your mouth, 'Jesus is Lord,' and believe in your heart that God raised him from the dead, you will be saved" (Romans 10:9, NIV).

"Salvation is found in no one else [Jesus], for there is no other name by which we must be saved" (Acts 4:12, NIV).

3. *Accept* God's free gift of salvation. Don't try to earn it.

"For it is by grace you have been saved, through faith—and this is not from yourselves, it is the gift of God—not by works, so that no one can boast" (Ephesians 2:8, 9, NIV).

"To all who received him, he gave the right to become children of God. All they needed to do was to trust him to save them. All those who believe this are reborn!—not a physical rebirth . . . but from the will of God" (John 1:12, 13, TLB).

Jesus says, "Here I am! I stand at the

door and knock. If anyone hears my voice and opens the door, I will come in . . ." (Revelation 3:20, NIV).

With all of my heart, I urge you to accept God's destiny for your life. I urge you to get on board with Christ. According to the Bible, "Jesus is the only One who can save people. His name is the only power in the world that has been given to save people. We must be saved through him" (Acts 4:12, NCV).

Would you let him save you? This is the most important decision you will ever make. Why don't you give your heart to him right now? *Admit* your need. *Agree* with his work. *Accept* his gift. Go to God in prayer and tell him, *I am a sinner in need of grace. I believe that Jesus died for me on the cross. I accept your offer of salvation.* It's a simple prayer with eternal results.

YOUR RESPONSE

I believe that Jesus Christ is the Son of the
Living God. I want him to be the Lord of
my life.

_____

Signed

_____

Date

Once you've placed your faith in Christ, I urge you to take three steps. You'll find them easy to remember. Just think of these three words. They each start with a "b": *baptism*, *Bible*, and *belonging*.

Baptism demonstrates and celebrates our decision to follow Jesus. The water of baptism symbolizes God's grace. Just as water cleanses the body, so grace cleanses the soul. Jesus said, "Anyone who believes and is baptized will be saved . . ." (Mark 16:16, NCV). When the apostle Paul became a believer, he was asked this question: "Now, why wait any longer? Get up, be baptized, and wash your sins away, trusting in him to save you" (Acts 22:16, NCV). Paul responded by being baptized immediately. You can, too.

Bible reading brings us face to face with God. God reveals himself to us through his word by the Holy Spirit. "Let the teaching of Christ live in you richly" (Colossians 3:16, NCV).

Belonging to a church reinforces your faith. A Christian without a church is like a baseball player without a team or a soldier without an army. You aren't strong enough to survive alone. "You should not stay away from the church meetings, as some are doing, but you should meet together and encourage each other" (Hebrews 10:25, NCV).

These three steps—baptism, Bible reading, and belonging to a church—are essential steps in your faith.

I pray that you'll accept this great gift of salvation. Believe me, this is not only the most important decision you'll ever make, it's also the greatest decision you'll ever make. There's no higher treasure than God's gift of salvation.

Postscript

HE DID THIS JUST FOR YOU

Postscript

HE DID THIS JUST FOR YOU

Want to know the coolest thing about the coming? Not that the One who played marbles with the stars gave it up to play marbles with marbles. Or that the One who hung the galaxies gave it up to hang doorjambs to the displeasure of a cranky client who wants everything yesterday but can't pay for anything until tomorrow.

Not that he, in an instant, went from needing nothing to needing air, food, a tub of hot water and salts for his tired feet, and

more than anything, needing somebody—
anybody—who was more concerned about
where they would spend eternity than
where they would spend Friday's paycheck.

Or that he resisted the urge to fry the
two-bit, self-appointed hall monitors of
holiness who dared suggest that he was
doing the work of the devil.

Not that he kept his cool while the
dozen best friends he never had felt the
heat and got out of the kitchen. Or that he
gave no command to the angels who
begged, "Just give the nod, Lord. One word
and these demons will be deviled eggs."

Not that he refused to defend himself
when blamed for every sin of every slut
and sailor since Adam. Or that he stood
silent as a million guilty verdicts echoed in
the tribunal of heaven, and the giver of
light was left in the chill of a sinner's night.

Not even that after three days in a dark
hole he stepped into the Easter sunrise
with a smile and a swagger and a question
for lowly Lucifer, "Is that your best
punch?"

That was cool, incredibly cool.

But want to know the coolest thing about the One who gave up the crown of heaven for a crown of thorns?

He did it for you. Just for you.

NOTES

1. "If you, then, though you are evil, know how to give good gifts to your children, how much more will your Father in heaven give good gifts to those who ask him!" (Matthew 7:11, NIV).

2. Frank Stagg, *New Testament Theology* (Nashville, Tenn: Broadman Press, 1962) 102.

ACKNOWLEDGMENT

To the Russian Christian who left a cross on my desk one Sunday a few years back: His note told how his newfound faith in Jesus led him to retrieve the nails from an old, abandoned Russian church. He formed the nails into a cross. Around the cross he wove a crown of barbed wire. This striking piece hangs on my office wall—and it also appears on the cover of this little book. My gratitude goes to the one whose name I do not know, but whose heart I do.

Max Lucado

ABOUT THE AUTHOR

MAX LUCADO is a preacher and writer who lives in San Antonio, Texas. He and his wife have three daughters. He is convinced that Jesus' promises are true and that the Easter sunrise will never fade. He speaks of his Savior each week at the Oak Hills Church of Christ and writes about him in his latest book, *He Chose the Nails*, from which much of the text for this small book is taken.

PERMISSIONS

References

All selections printed by permission of the publisher. All rights reserved.

"The Parable" is taken from *He Chose the Nails* (Nashville, Tenn.: W Publishing Group, 2000), 54–56, 59–68.

"The Promise" is taken from *He Chose the Nails* (Nashville, Tenn.: W Publishing Group, 2000), 112–115.

"The Privilege" is taken from *The Gift for All People* (Sisters, Orego: Multnomah Publishers, 1999), 127–135.

"Postscript" is taken from *He Chose the Nails* (Nashville, Tenn.: W Publishing Group, 2000), 26–27.